PARROTS, MACAWS, AND COCKATOOS

Harry N. Abrams, Inc., Publishers

Parrots, Macaws, and Cockatoos

The Art of Elizabeth Butterworth

Project Director: Barbara Lyons
Editor: Mark D. Greenberg
Designer: Carol A. Robson

On the cover: Scarlet Macaw (see page 24)

On the title page: Umbrella Cockatoo (see page 62)

On the back cover: Tropical House with Scarlet Macaw [detail] (see page 52)

Library of Congress Cataloging-in-Publication Data
Butterworth, Elizabeth.
    Parrots, macaws, and cockatoos: the art of Elizabeth Butterworth.
       p.   cm.
    ISBN 0—8109—2585—0
    1. Butterworth, Elizabeth.   2. Parrots in art.   3. Macaws in art.
  4. Cockatoos in art.   I. Title.
  N6797.B9A4 1988
  760′.092′4—dc19   87-24525
                                                              CIP

This 1994 edition published by Harry N. Abrams, Incorporated, New York
A Times Mirror Company

Printed and bound in Japan

TO JERRY

I am indebted to the following friends and authors,
who have given me
a better understanding of this subject:
Wendy Dougan,
Rodolphe d'Erlanger,
Daphne Grunebaum,
John Halford,
Rosemary Low,
George Smith,
and Joseph Forshaw
for his book
Parrots of the World.

Largely because of their "colorful talk" parrots have held a high place in man's affection since ancient times. My introduction to them was in 1972 when, in my final year of studying painting at London's Royal College of Art, my boyfriend bought me a Scarlet Macaw. The bird and I lived side by side in my studio, and we soon became friends. It was some time later, while searching for subject matter, that I decided to do some drawings of the macaw—and so it all began.

At the time, my knowledge of these birds was very limited, but with these first drawings came a desire to discover more. I was struck by the size and variety of the parrot family, ranging from the Pygmy Parrot (*Micropsittinae*) of New Guinea, which weighs less than half an ounce (about the size of a wren), to the huge Hyacinthine Macaw (*Anodorhynchus hyacinthinus*) from South America, which is three feet long and weighs over three pounds, not to mention the cockatoos with their rising crests, and the kakapo, the heaviest of all and the only flightless member of the family.

Parrots are distributed throughout the torrid zone, from the tropic of Cancer to the tropic of Capricorn. The northern boundary, set by the recently extinct Carolina Conure (*Conuropsis [Aratinga] carolinensis*), extended from Florida to the North American Great Lakes; the southern boundary is set by the Austral Conure (*Enicognathus ferrugineus*), which inhabits Tierra del Fuego off the southern tip of South America. Within these boundaries, the most diverse species are found in Australia, the greatest number in South America, and a scattering in Africa and India.

At present about three hundred species are recognized. I say "about" because they are continually being recategorized by those who like to arrange, relate, and tidy up species of birds. Count Tomasso Salvadori first categorized them for the British Museum in 1896, and his system has remained the basis for further revisions. Categories are generally based on physical appearance and anatomy, however the latest classification by Dr. Dominique G. Homberger, in *The Dictionary of Birds*, is greatly influenced by how parrots feed and drink, but this system will probably not satisfy everybody.

It was not until I started work on *Parrots and Cockatoos* (London, 1978), in collaboration with Rosemary Low, that I discovered the appalling plight of many birds in the wild. Parrots that are exclusive to small oceanic islands and those with limited ranges on the mainland have become endangered, and seven species have become extinct in recent times. It is ironic that man, supposedly the parrots' best friend, has also proved to be their most effective destroyer. The indiscriminate use of pesticides and herbicides and dealers' profiteering have undoubtedly helped to put many species on the endangered list, but it is the loss of habitat that has proved to be the greatest evil. A few, however, including three species of Australian cockatoo

and the Indian Ringnecked Parakeet (*Psittacula krameri*), have so increased in number as to be considered pests.

With the exception of the kakapo and some keas (*Nestor notabilis*), both from New Zealand, parrots are believed to be monogamous, pairing for life. The pair bond is maintained by mutual preening, shared roosting, copulation, and courtship feeding. A breeding pair of my cockatoos (*Cacatua sulphurea citrinocristata*) can often be seen "rubbing shoulders." They mate frequently throughout the year. This is generally preceded by the male strutting up and down the perch with his crest raised and wings and tail spread showing their yellow undersides. He will bob and sway his head, preen the female excitedly, then strut off to repeat the courtship several times. The hen, understandably impressed and excited by such foreplay, crouches low on the perch quivering with anticipation. The male, after a few tentative prods on her back with his foot, will then step on her, steadying himself by holding her nape feathers with his beak, and finally, wrapping his tail under hers, copulates.

Hawk Headed Parrot, 1975
Pen and ink, 12 x 1 1 ½"
Collection the artist

Pesquet Parrot, 1975
Pen and ink, 10½ x 9″
Collection the artist

The majority of parrots nest in holes in trees. A few excavate holes in termitaria, and keas use "caves" between rocks, which they dig out partially themselves. The Quaker Parakeet (*Myiopsitta monachus*) is the only one to build a nest in the branches of trees. During my visit to the Mato Grosso, in southeastern Brazil, I saw trees festooned with these nests—large trees may carry as many as six. These gregarious little birds build nests in colonies, each pair building a chamber onto the last, and the result is a mass of twigs about the size of a small car with the entrance holes in the underside, presumably as protection against predators.

The number of eggs laid varies roughly in inverse proportion to the size of bird, the smaller parrots laying up to eight and the large macaws two and sometimes three. The white eggs are laid every other day and hatch after eighteen to twenty-nine days according to the size of the bird. With the exception of cockatoos, who share incubation and chick brooding, the female incubates alone. The young fledge after about twelve weeks for cockatoos and fourteen weeks for macaws. The parents will continue to feed them for a short time, and in the wild the young will often stay as a family group until the following breeding season. In captivity, it is thought wise to remove the young once they are self-sufficient as the parents can become aggressive toward them in an enclosed space.

I hope that these notes give some idea of the diversity within the parrot family. The conservation of these wonderful birds is a subject that is very close to me. The trade in them has grown into a large and profitable international business, fueled by the increasing demand for rare birds and the scarcity of these from home breeders. Of the thousands of parrots that are captured each year, only a tiny proportion reach the customer alive. Both the Candinde Macaw (*Ara caninde*) and the Red-fronted Macaw (*Ara rubrogenys*) have become endangered through trapping, the latter's range having been discovered only in 1973.

Fortunately, some countries have banned the export of birds, and were this coupled with a worldwide ban on imports, the problem might be contained. For those birds whose environment has been destroyed the solution would be to distribute captive breeding stock among selected aviculturalists, who would be permitted to import and export limited numbers to facilitate the exchange of new blood.

E. Butterworth.

London, 1987

Moluccan Cockatoo, 1978
Oil on canvas, 14 x 11"
Private collection

The Plates

Green Morph, Guilding's Amazon

1981

Gouache and watercolor, 11 ½ x 9 ½"

Private collection

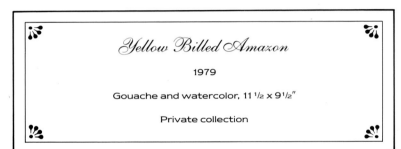

Yellow Billed Amazon

1979

Gouache and watercolor, 11 $\frac{1}{2}$ x 9 $\frac{1}{2}$"

Private collection

Red Tailed Amazon

1981

Gouache and watercolor, 11 ½ x 9½"

Private collection

Yellow Cheeked Amazon

1980

Gouache and watercolor, 11 ½ x 9½″

Private collection

Blue Fronted Amazon

1981

Gouache and watercolor, 11 ½ x 9½"

Private collection

Sketches of Amazon Parrots

1980

Pen and ink, gouache, and watercolor, 20 x 30″

Private collection

Sketches of Amazon Parrots

1980

Pen and ink, gouache, and watercolor, 20 x 30″

Private collection

Scarlet Macaw

1984

Gouache, 31 x 21"

Collection the artist

Green Winged Macaw

1985

Gouache, 31 x 21"

Collection the artist

Sketch of Blue and Gold Macaw

1985

Pen and ink and gouache, 12½ x 7¾"

Collection the artist

A. Ararauna.

Sketch of Hyacynthine Macaw

1984

Pen and ink and gouache, 20¹⁄₂ x 15¹⁄₂″

Collection the artist

Immature Bird   84 - Captive?
No Yellow Stripe on tongue
Tail Shorter.

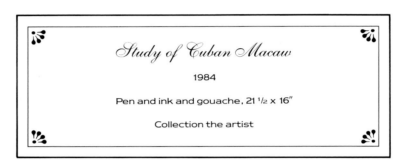

Study of Cuban Macaw

1984

Pen and ink and gouache, 21 ½ x 16"

Collection the artist

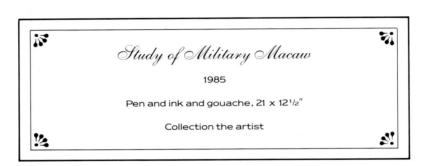

Study of Military Macaw

1985

Pen and ink and gouache, 21 x 12¹⁄₂"

Collection the artist

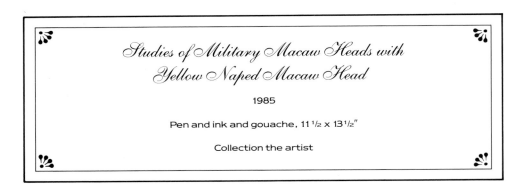

Studies of Military Macaw Heads with
Yellow Naped Macaw Head

1985

Pen and ink and gouache, 11 ½ x 13 ½"

Collection the artist

Studies of Green Winged Macaw

1985

Pencil and gouache, 11 ½ x 12¾"

Collection the artist

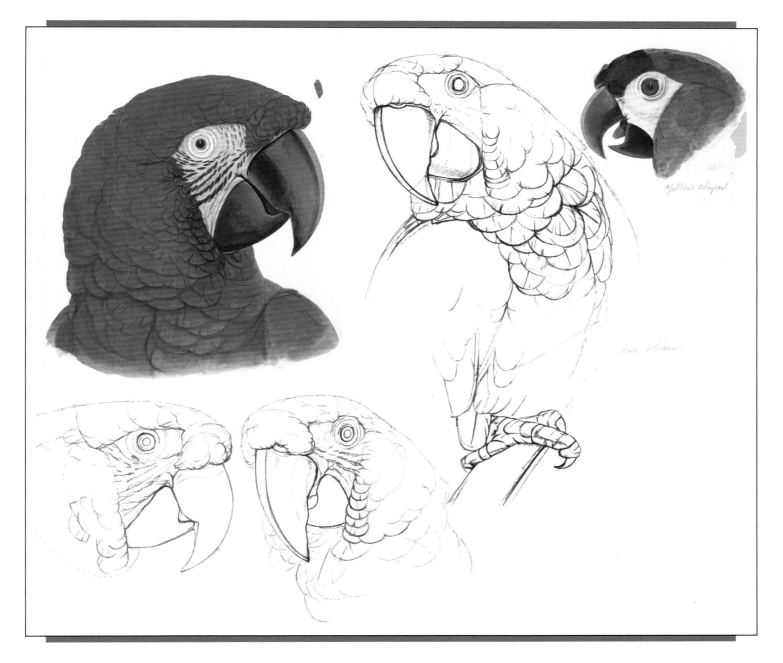

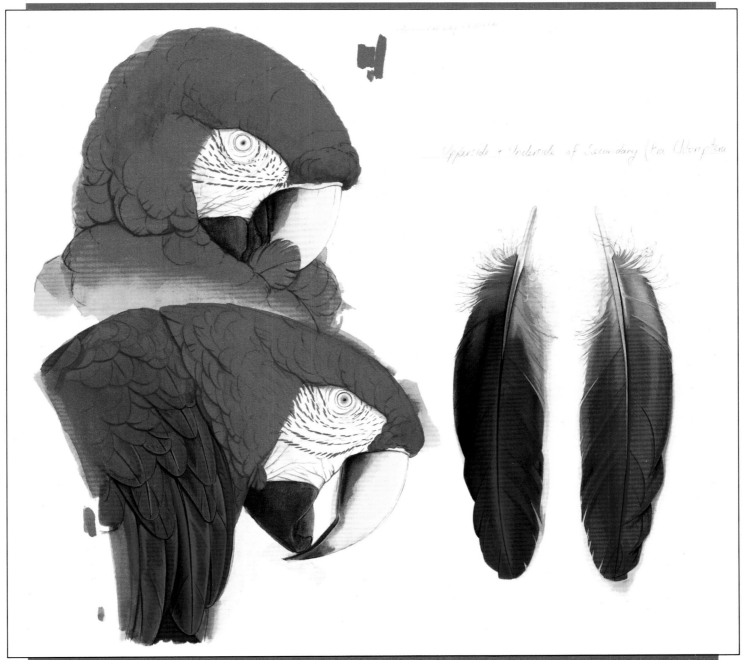

Military Macaw with Buffon's Macaw Head

1986

Gouache, 31 x 21"

Collection the artist

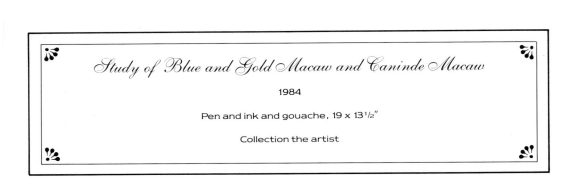

Study of Blue and Gold Macaw and Caninde Macaw

1984

Pen and ink and gouache, 19 x 13¹/₂″

Collection the artist

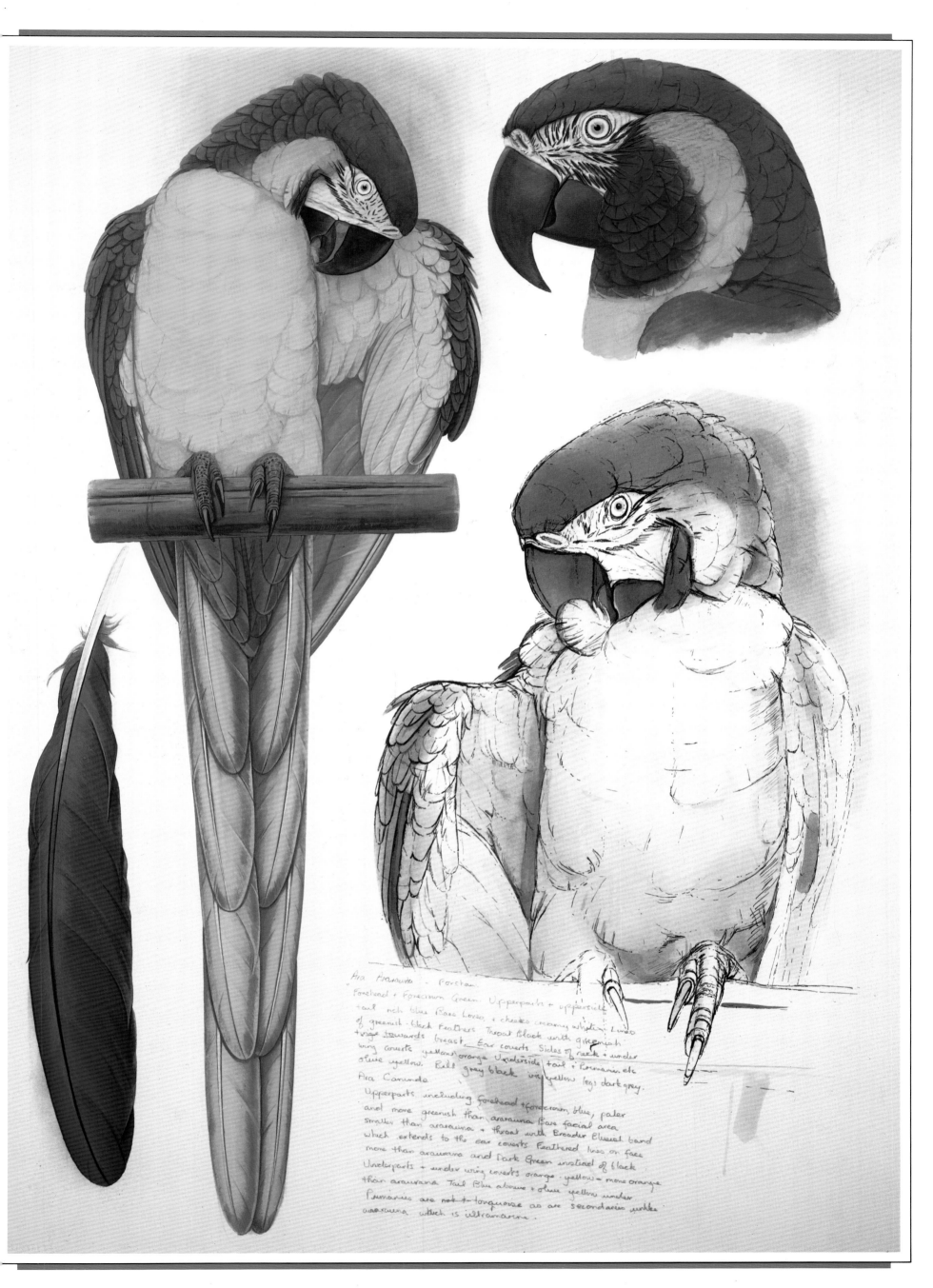

Ara Araraura - Forstan

Forehead + Forecrown Green. Upperparts + upperside
tail rich blue Bare Lores + cheeks creamy whitish Lines
of greenish-black feathers Throat Black with greenish
tinge towards breast. Ear coverts Sides of neck + under
wing coverts yellow/orange Underside tail + Primaries etc
olive yellow. Bill grey black with yellow legs dark grey.

Ara Caninde

Upperparts, including forehead +forecrown blue, paler
and more greenish than araraura Bare facial area
smaller than araraura + throat with Broader Blueish band
which extends to the ear coverts Feathered lines on face
more than araraura and dark Green instead of black
Underparts + under wing coverts orange-yellow - more orange
than araraura Tail Blue above + olive yellow under
Primaries are not t-torquoise as are secondaries unlike
araraura which is ultramarine.

Spix Macaw

1986

Gouache, 19¹/₂ x 13¹/₂"

Collection the artist

Spix Macaw   Cyanopsitta spixii

Lears and Glaucous Macaw

1986

Gouache, 31 x 21"

Collection the artist

Blue and Gold Macaw

1984

Gouache, 31 x 21"

Collection the artist

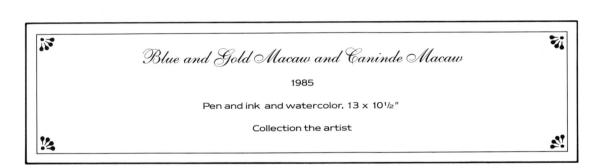

Blue and Gold Macaw and Caninde Macaw

1985

Pen and ink and watercolor, 13 x 10½"

Collection the artist

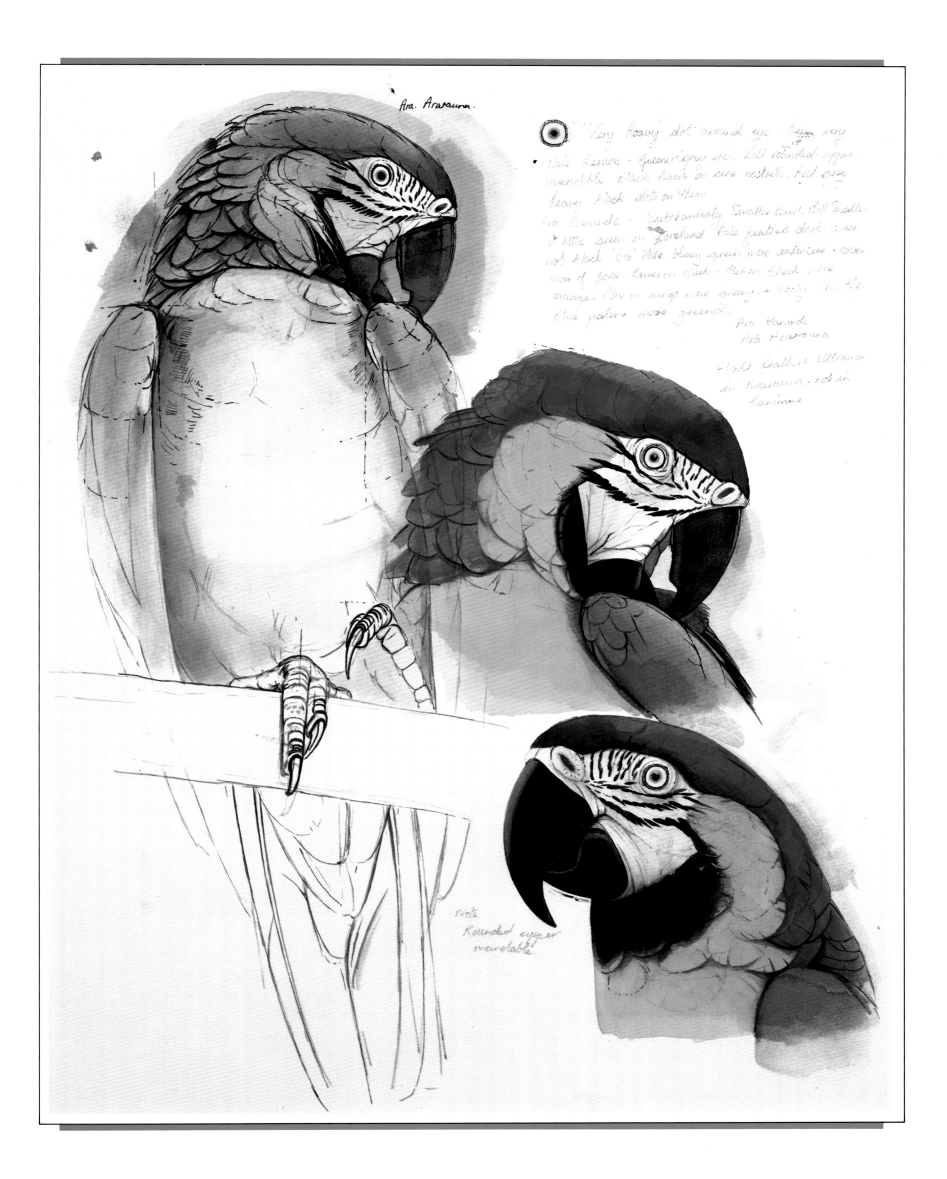

Underside and Upperside Wing of Bronze Winged Pionus Parrot

1982

Gouache and watercolor, 17 1/2 x 12 1/2"

Private collection

Tropical House with Scarlet Macaw

1978

Oil and acrylic on canvas, 36 x 24"

Private collection

Citron Crested Cockatoo with Wing Studies

1982

Gouache and watercolor, 23³/₄ x 27³/₄"

Private collection

Citron Crested Cockatoo

1982

Pen and ink, gouache, and watercolor, 23³/₄ x 28"

Private collection

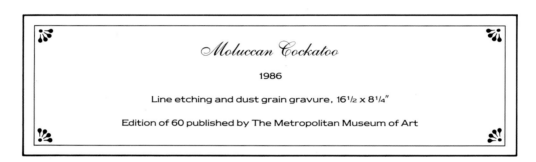

Moluccan Cockatoo

1986

Line etching and dust grain gravure, 16½ x 8¼″

Edition of 60 published by The Metropolitan Museum of Art

Leadbeater's Cockatoo Wing Studies

1987

Gouache, 21 ½ x 15 ½"

Collection the artist

Moluccan Cockatoo

1982

Watercolor, 29 x 21 ½"

Private collection

Umbrella Cockatoo

1978

Gouache and watercolor, 7 ½ x 7"

Private collection